NATIONAL GEOGRAPHIC KiDS

W9-ATF-829

Funny FiLL-IN

MY INSIDE THE EARTH ADVENTURE

NATIONAL GEOGRAPHIC
WASHINGTON, D.C.

How to Play Funny Fill-In!

Love to create amazing stories? Good, because this one stars YOU. Get ready to laugh with all your friends—you can play with as many people as you want! Make sure to keep this book on your shelf. You'll want to read it again and again!

Are You Ready to Laugh?

- One person picks a story—you can start at the beginning, the middle, or the end of the book.

- Ask a friend to call out a word that the space asks for—noun, verb, or something else—and write it in the blank space. If there's more than one player, ask the next person to say a word. Extra points for creativity!

- When all the spaces are filled in, you have your very own Funny Fill-In. Read it out loud for a laugh.

- Want to play by yourself? Just fold over the page and use the cardboard insert at the back as a writing pad. Fill in the blank parts of speech list, and copy your answers into the story.

Fun Fact!

Make sure you check out the amazing **Fun Facts** that appear on every page!

To play the game, you'll need to know how to form sentences. This list with examples of the parts of speech and other terms will help you get started:

Noun: The name of a person, place, thing, or idea
Examples: tree, mouth, creature
*The **ocean** is full of colorful **fish.***

Adjective: A word that describes a noun or pronoun
Examples: green, lazy, friendly
*My **silly** dog won't stop laughing!*

Verb: An action word. In the present tense, a verb often ends in –s or –ing. If the space asks for past tense, changing the vowel or adding a –d or –ed to the end usually will set the sentence in the past.
Examples: swim, hide, plays, running (present tense); biked, rode, jumped (past tense)
*The giraffe **skips** across the savanna.*
*The flower **opened** after the rain.*

Adverb: A word that describes a verb and usually ends in –ly
Examples: quickly, lazily, soundlessly
*Kelley **greedily** ate all the carrots.*

Plural: More than one
Examples: mice, telephones, wrenches
*Why are all the **doors** closing?*

Silly Word or Exclamation: A funny sound, a made-up word, a word you think is totally weird, or a noise someone or something might make
Examples: Ouch! No way! Foozleduzzle! Yikes!
*"**Darn!**" shouted Jim. "These cupcakes are sour!"*

Specific Words: There are many more ways to make your story hilarious. When asked for something like a number, animal, or body part, write in something you think is especially funny.

- friend's name
- silly word
- noun, plural
- verb ending in –s
- large number
- adjective
- noun, plural
- adjective
- liquid
- exclamation
- noun
- same liquid
- noun, plural
- adjective
- same friend's name
- verb ending in –ing
- verb
- animal
- verb ending in –ing

Fun Fact! A PERSON WHO EXPLORES **CAVES** IS CALLED A **SPELUNKER.**

4

Creepy Cave

It's so cool that _____ and I are partners for our class science project! Today we're
friend's name

hiking through _____ National Park to take photos of _____ and write about
silly word _noun, plural_

what _____ here. So far we have _____ pictures of the dirt path and one
verb ending in –s _large number_

_____ photo of some _____ . We're deep in the woods when _____
adjective _noun, plural_ _adjective_

clouds form above and _____ begins to pour from the sky. "_____!" I shout. We
liquid _exclamation_

look around for a(n) _____ to wait out the storm. Just then, _____ washes
noun _same liquid_

away _____ covering the opening to a cave. We go inside to dry off, but something feels
noun, plural

_____ in here. "Shh, do you hear that?" _____ asks. We listen to an odd
adjective _same friend's name_

_____ sound coming from the shadows. I _____ around and hope it's just
verb ending in –ing _verb_

a(n) _____ _____ .
animal _verb ending in –ing_

Fun Fact!

CAVE DRAWINGS
OF HANDS FOUND IN SPAIN ARE MORE THAN 40,000 YEARS OLD.

- friend's name
- noun, plural
- adjective
- adjective
- animal
- verb ending in –ing
- electronic gadget
- noun, plural
- a profession
- verb
- historical figure
- sea animal
- noun
- piece of furniture
- same friend's name
- clothing item
- verb ending in –s

Wall of Weird

_____ and I hold our _____ and listen to the _____
     friend's name   noun, plural   adjective

noise in the dimly lit cave. I look down at the _____ rock we're sitting on and see a drawing
                                                              adjective

of a fuzzy _____ _____. How odd, I think. I click on my _____
              animal   verb ending in –ing   electronic gadget

and shine it on the surrounding _____. Whoa, there are drawings all over the place!
                                        noun, plural

A(n) _____ must have done these! When I _____ closer to check out a drawing
        a profession   verb

of _____ riding a(n) _____, the noise gets louder and closer.
     historical figure   sea animal

Suddenly, a troll appears from the shadows holding a(n) _____ and dragging a heavy
                                                              noun

_____ behind him. _____ and I scream and grab each
     piece of furniture   same friend's name

other's _____. The troll _____ up and down and exclaims, "Yay!
           clothing item   verb ending in –s

I'm happy you're as excited about my art gallery as I am!"

7

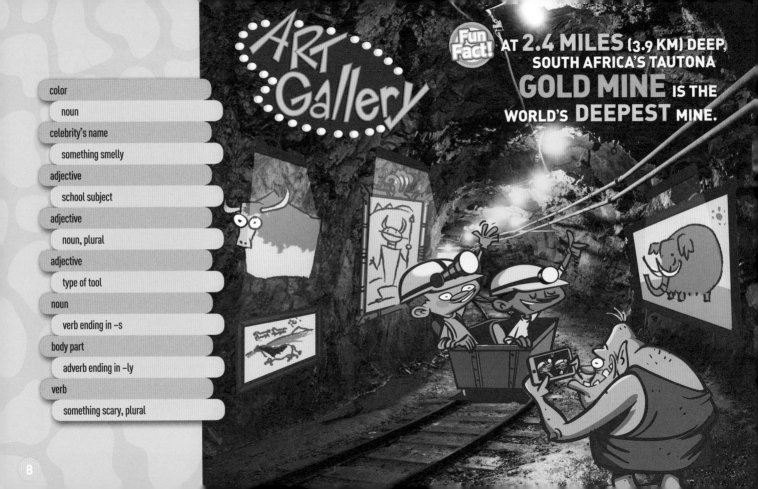

Art Gallery

- color
  - noun
- celebrity's name
  - something smelly
- adjective
  - school subject
- adjective
  - noun, plural
- adjective
  - type of tool
- noun
  - verb ending in –s
- body part
  - adverb ending in –ly
- verb
  - something scary, plural

Fun Fact! AT **2.4 MILES** (3.9 KM) DEEP, SOUTH AFRICA'S TAUTONA **GOLD MINE** IS THE WORLD'S **DEEPEST** MINE.

The troll pushes a(n) _____ (color) button on the wall and a(n) _____ (noun) lights up that says

"_____ (celebrity's name) 's Gallery of _____ (something smelly) Art." He tells us that these are all

_____ (adjective) artworks that show the _____ (school subject) research he has done deep in the cave.

He's now retired and runs this gallery to keep _____ (adjective) . But since it's so hidden, he doesn't get a

lot of _____ (noun, plural) . I bet! He offers to take a photo of us in the _____ (adjective) mining cart he

used for his research. We jump in and hold up his mining _____ (type of tool) . The troll steps back to get

the _____ (noun) in the photo and accidentally _____ (verb ending in –s) on the release lever. Luckily, I

catch the camera as it flies out of his _____ (body part) , but the mining cart is _____ (adverb ending in –ly) rolling

down the tracks into the cave! The troll yells after us, "_____ (verb) away from the—" We're gone

before we hear the rest. I hope he wasn't going to say "_____ (something scary, plural) "!

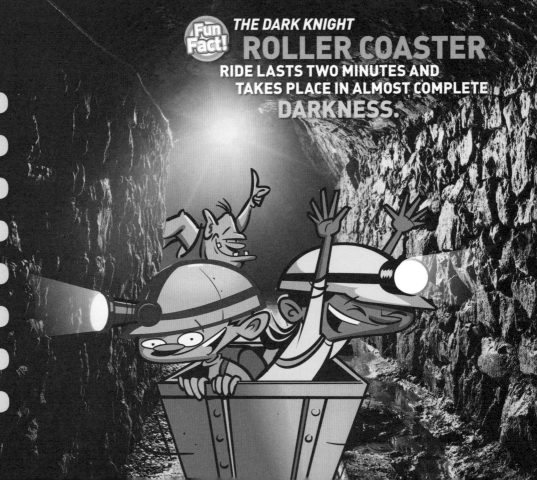

THE DARK KNIGHT
ROLLER COASTER
RIDE LASTS TWO MINUTES AND
TAKES PLACE IN ALMOST COMPLETE
DARKNESS.

- body part, plural
- verb
- adjective
- direction
- verb
- noun
- favorite roller coaster
- verb ending in –ing
- silly word
- adjective
- same silly word
- friend's name
- verb ending in –s
- body part
- adverb ending in –ly
- favorite color

Into the Darkness

We grip the mining cart tightly with our _____ as it zooms deeper into the cave.
<u>body part, plural</u>

I _____, bracing myself against the _____ air hitting my face. The cart turns
<u>verb</u> <u>adjective</u>

_____, then makes a sharp right. We ride upward, then _____ down and spin into
<u>direction</u> <u>verb</u>

a(n) _____. Wow, this is just like riding the _____! Too bad we can't see
<u>noun</u> <u>favorite roller coaster</u>

where we're _____. "_____!" I shout. My voice echoes back, followed by
<u>verb ending in –ing</u> <u>silly word</u>

a(n) _____ echo from somewhere in the cave. "_____!" we hear over and over.
<u>adjective</u> <u>same silly word</u>

Then _____ and I hear laughing. Who or what is laughing? "What's so funny?" I shout.
<u>friend's name</u>

"You!" the voice _____ back. I feel something brush past my _____ and land
<u>verb ending in –s</u> <u>body part</u>

_____ in the cart with us. We turn around and see a creature with _____
<u>adverb ending in –ly</u> <u>favorite color</u>

glowing eyes staring back at us. It's my favorite color, but it definitely doesn't look good now!

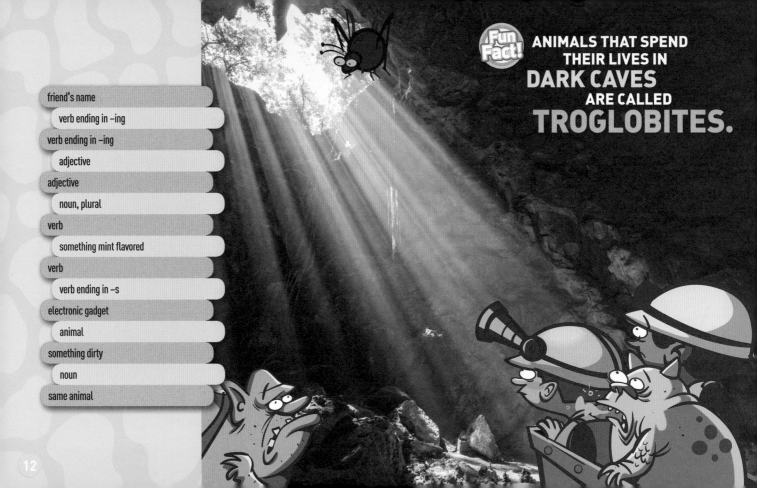

friend's name

verb ending in –ing

verb ending in –ing

adjective

adjective

noun, plural

verb

something mint flavored

verb

verb ending in –s

electronic gadget

animal

something dirty

noun

same animal

Fun Fact! ANIMALS THAT SPEND THEIR LIVES IN **DARK CAVES** ARE CALLED **TROGLOBITES.**

Goofy Guest

_____ and I are _____ out! I can't decide what's scarier: _____
(friend's name)   (verb ending in –ing)   (verb ending in –ing)

backward into a(n) _____ cave or the creature with _____ eyes staring at us.
                        (adjective)   (adjective)

Just when we are wishing we could grow _____ and _____ away from here, the
                                            (noun, plural)   (verb)

mysterious creature burps. What a stink! Has this thing never heard of _____ ?
                                                                            (something mint flavored)

"We should at least see what's about to _____ us," I whisper. My hand _____
                                            (verb)   (verb ending in –s)

as I switch on my _____ . We're stunned. The creature is a cute _____ ! But
                    (electronic gadget)   (animal)

boy, its breath smells like _____ . "I've been waiting for a(n) _____ out of
                            (something dirty)   (noun)

here," the _____ says. Ahead we see light streaming through a sinkhole in the top of the
            (same animal)

cave. A shadowy figure sits in the corner. With one creature above and one in the cart, we're not sure this

ride could get any crazier. Boy, were we wrong.

friend's name

adjective

something sharp, plural

adjective

verb

noun

lucky number

adjective

same friend's name

verb

adjective

something sticky

verb ending in –s

adverb ending in –ly

Fun Fact! WEAVERS IN MADAGASCAR CREATED A RARE **TAPESTRY** MADE ENTIRELY OF **SPIDER SILK.**

Rappelling Rescue

"Let's keep this ride moving!" _____ says. But with the extra weight in the cart, we
                                   friend's name

come to a stop high above the ground. Suddenly, the shadow of a creature with _____ legs and
                                                                                  adjective

two _____ appears above us. Something _____ and wet hits my face. Creature
     something sharp, plural   adjective

drool! It's hungry, and we're dinner—a la carte! Maybe we can _____ down to the cave floor. I
                                                                  verb

toss a(n) _____ to gauge how high up we are. We listen for _____ minutes
           noun   lucky number

before we hear it hit the bottom. Uh oh. The creature gets right in our faces and says, "Need some help?"

Whew! It's a(n) _____ spider! _____ and I use the spider's silk to rappel to
                 adjective   same friend's name

the cave floor and _____. The silk is _____ and feels like _____.
                    verb   adjective   something sticky

"All fixed!" the spider shouts from above as it _____ down after us and _____
                                                 verb ending in –s   adverb ending in –ly

lands beside us on the cave floor. Our hero!

friend's name

sport

adjective

number

favorite board game

type of dessert

same friend's name

body part

something noisy

adjective

animal, plural

small number

sea creature, plural

adjective

noun, plural

something fast

body part

Fun Fact!

AT THE
BATHTUB REGATTA
IN BELGIUM, PARTICIPANTS RACE IN
BATHTUBS AND OTHER
HOMEMADE FLOATS.

FINISH

Our new friend the giant spider asks _____ and me to join his _____ team
friend's name _sport_

in a(n) _____ race. But the rules are really strange: We have to play _____ rounds
adjective _number_

of _____ while paddling across an underground lake. Piece of _____ !
favorite board game _type of dessert_

Our boat is tiny, so I have to sit on _____'s _____ . A(n) _____
same friend's name _body part_ _something noisy_

toots and it's a(n) _____ dash to the finish line! A boat with albino _____ pulls
adjective _animal, plural_

into the lead. Then we're passed by _____ blind _____ riding in a
small number _sea creature, plural_

submarine. That seems a little _____ . But then I realize our team easily has more legs and
adjective

_____ than the competition. We paddle like a(n) _____ and sail
noun, plural _something fast_

through the finish line to take first place! Now that's putting your best _____
body part

forward! Ahead, we see a cavern with flashing lights.

1st Place

- adjective
  - friend's name
- verb ending in –s
  - verb ending in –s
- same friend's name
  - musical instrument
- adjective
  - type of rock
- horn instrument
  - musical instrument
- noun, plural
  - fictional character
- adjective ending in –est
  - favorite song
- exclamation
  - verb
- same friend's name
  - noun, plural

Fun Fact! THE GREAT STALACPIPE ORGAN, IN LURAY CAVERNS, VIRGINIA, U.S.A., IS THE WORLD'S **LARGEST MUSICAL INSTRUMENT.**

A large crowd is gathering and lights are flashing outside a(n) _____ cavern. _____ and I decide to
                                                              adjective   *friend's name*

check out the action. As we step inside, a rock band bursts into song. Everyone _____ and _____
                                                                                 verb ending in –s   *verb ending in –s*

to the beat. _____ and I are extra excited because we both play the _____ in our school
             same friend's name   *musical instrument*

band. But this concert is unlike anything we've ever seen. All the instruments are made of _____
                                                                                            adjective

minerals from the cave itself. There's a(n) _____ guitar and a copper _____ . Plus, a huge
                                             type of rock   *horn instrument*

_____ is carved directly into the cave wall, and it vibrates the _____ all around us.
musical instrument   *noun, plural*

We dance like we're _____ while the band plays the _____ metal songs of all time.
                    fictional character   *adjective ending in –est*

"Play '_____ '!" I shout, but the singer doesn't know it. "_____ !" I cry, jumping onstage with
       favorite song   *exclamation*

the band and grabbing a microphone. I _____ out the lyrics while _____ drums on a set
                                       verb   *same friend's name*

of steel _____ . This must be where rock and roll got started!
         noun, plural

- friend's name
- pop star
- verb ending in –ing
- noun, plural
- adjective
- type of dance
- gymnastic move, plural
- adjective ending in –er
- shape
- animal
- adjective
- relative's name
- barnyard animal
- past-tense verb
- somewhere smelly
- same friend's name
- verb
- body part, plural
- adjective

Fun Fact!

HONEYBEES, PEACOCK SPIDERS, AND EVEN ALGAE "DANCE" TO COMMUNICATE OR TO REPRODUCE.

Flash Mob!

_____ and I are rocking on stage like we're _____ ! We look at the
   friend's name   pop star

cheering crowd and see tons of ants _____ into the concert hall. All at once, they look at their
                                     verb ending in –ing

_____ and break into a synchronized dance. It's a flash mob! These ants are _____
   noun, plural   adjective

dancers. They know _____ and can even do _____ without missing a beat.
                  type of dance   gymnastic move, plural

It gets _____ when they climb on each other to build a super _____ . Together they
    adjective ending in –er   shape

look like a giant _____ dancing the cha-cha! I haven't seen a performance this _____
               animal   adjective

since _____ tripped on the family _____ and they both _____ into
   relative's name   barnyard animal   past-tense verb

the _____ . _____ and I slide into line with the ants. First we wiggle to
   somewhere smelly   same friend's name

the left, next we _____ our big toes, and then we hop on the tip of our _____ .
              verb   body part, plural

I can't wait to teach the dance to everyone at school. This is sure to be the next _____ trend!
                                                                               adjective

- friend's name
- adjective
- verb
- beverage
- type of building
- noun
- type of important person
- large number
- adjective
- noun
- large animal, plural
- favorite video game
- animal, plural
- type of transportation, plural
- verb ending in –ing
- verb ending in –s
- favorite snack

Fun Fact!

A GROUP OF **ANTS** BUILT A **SUPERCOLONY** THAT SPANS **3,700** MILES (6,000 KM).

Sisterhood of the Traveling Ants

Cool Colony

Trying to keep up with dancing ants makes _____ and me really _____ .
                                              friend's name   adjective

Fortunately, the ants _____ us back to their colony for _____ and a snack. But first
                          verb   beverage

they insist on giving us a tour of their underground _____ . Wow, this place is a(n)
                                                           type of building

_____ fit for a(n) _____ . There are _____ levels, with everything
       noun   type of important person   large number

you could need or want. The ants show us the theater that only plays _____ movies. There's a
                                                                          adjective

bouncy _____ that fits up to six _____ . Next to that is the arcade, where you can
            noun   large animal, plural

play _____ starting on any level you want. The ants even have an aquarium full of
       favorite video game

undiscovered sea _____ . My favorite room, though, is the bumper _____
                      animal, plural   type of transportation, plural

arena. We ride around, _____ into each other until my stomach _____ .
                          verb ending in –ing   verb ending in –s

The ants offer us some mold to eat, but we politely decline. We'd rather find _____ !
                                                                                  favorite snack

23

friend's name

snack food, plural

adjective

adjective

something weird, plural

body part

U.S. state

dessert

relative's name

day of the week

adjective

large number

food beginning with the letter "P"

adjective

verb

noun

same U.S. state

something gross

noun

Fun Fact! A RESTAURANT IN JAPAN SERVES A WHOLE MEAL FEATURING DIRT—TOPPED OFF WITH DIRT ICE CREAM!

It's been hours since _____ and I ate our _____ back in the woods.
friend's name   snack food, plural

Thankfully, we find an underground diner packed with customers. This place must be _____ !
adjective

The menu has a lot of _____ choices, like leafy salads and all-natural _____ . But
adjective   something weird, plural

what really catches my _____ is the _____ mud pie. The photo of it looks like my
body part   U.S. state

favorite chocolate _____ that _____ makes every _____ . I'm so
dessert   relative's name   day of the week

_____ to eat the pie that I ask for _____ orders of it. But just in case that's not enough, I
adjective   large number

order a side of dirty _____ . When the dishes arrive, they look even more _____
food beginning with the letter "P"   adjective

than they do in the menu pictures. I can't wait to _____ in! I scoop a large _____-ful of
verb   noun

the _____ mud pie into my mouth. It tastes like a(n) _____ . We spit everything
same U.S. state   something gross

out and wipe our tongues on the _____ . What a dirty surprise!
noun

- friend's name
  - noun, plural
- verb ending in –ing
  - adjective ending in –est
- adjective
  - small number
- color
  - animal
- adjective
  - body part, plural
- verb ending in –s
  - noun, plural
- verb
  - cartoon character
- verb
  - same friend's name
- famous athlete
  - verb
- adjective ending in –est

Fun Fact!

THE TEXAS BLIND SALAMANDER FINDS ITS PREY BY SENSING CHANGES IN WATER PRESSURE.

_____ and I run into a group of odd-looking creatures that are sawing _____
(friend's name)   (noun, plural)

and _____ clay. They are definitely the _____ bunch down here. Each
(verb ending in –ing)   (adjective ending in –est)

one has a(n) _____ body with _____ toe(s), a long _____ tail, and
(adjective)   (small number)   (color)

a giant head like a(n) _____ . We're surprised that they are so _____ at sculpting
(animal)   (adjective)

because they don't have any eyes. Instead, they use their _____ to feel how something
(body part, plural)

_____ . We ask them to teach us how they create the beautiful _____ . First,
(verb ending in –s)   (noun, plural)

one will _____ like _____ while the others _____ . Then they switch
(verb)   (cartoon character)   (verb)

places. _____ and I pose like _____ and ask them if they'll
(same friend's name)   (famous athlete)

carve a sculpture of us. They _____ with excitement and say, "Of course! You two are by far
(verb)

the _____ things in this cave!"
(adjective ending in –est)

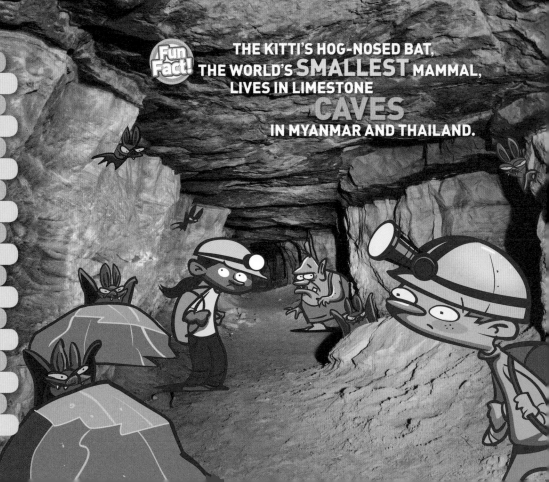

adjective
_____

type of athlete, plural
_____

friend's name
_____

noun, plural
_____

silly word
_____

verb ending in –ing
_____

small number
_____

noun
_____

beverage
_____

adjective
_____

adverb ending in –ly
_____

same friend's name
_____

past-tense verb
_____

verb
_____

adjective
_____

noun
_____

adjective
_____

favorite game
_____

Fun Fact!

THE KITTI'S HOG-NOSED BAT,
THE WORLD'S SMALLEST MAMMAL,
LIVES IN LIMESTONE
CAVES
IN MYANMAR AND THAILAND.

Bat Battle

We're deep in the cave when suddenly a couple of _____ (adjective) bats swoop overhead like aerial

_____ (type of athlete, plural). "Duck!" _____ (friend's name) shouts. We soon discover they're competing in a series

of _____ (noun, plural). It's like field day at school, except down here it's called _____ (silly word) Day.

The bats challenge us to the next event: ringtoss. Luckily, I've been practicing my _____ (verb ending in –ing) skills since

I was _____ (small number). Did I mention I also have an excellent sense of _____ (noun)? As for the bats,

well, let's just say ringtoss is not their cup of _____ (beverage). Their wingspans are too _____ (adjective),

and they can't even throw _____ (adverb ending in –ly). _____ (same friend's name) and I win this event, but the bats

_____ (past-tense verb) us in the next event: hide-and-_____ (verb). Not only did they already know all

the _____ (adjective) spots, they could hear us crawling into a hiding _____ (noun). It's a tie game when

we all agree to join together in a(n) _____ (adjective) game of _____ (favorite game) instead.

body part

adjective

friend's name

verb

pattern

animal

number

exotic location

adjective

large number

adverb ending in –ly

something gooey

type of chore

adjective

verb

clothing item, plural

liquid

type of swim

"SODA STRAWS" AND "BACON STRIPS" ARE NAMES FOR STALACTITE FORMATIONS.

Tubular Tour

I wipe the sweat off my _____ . Exploring caves is _____ work! We arrive at an
                          body part   adjective

underground river, and _____ suggests we join a river tour. So I _____ into a(n)
                        friend's name   verb

_____ inner tube in the shape of a(n) _____ and link it up to the rest of the group. Our
   pattern   animal

guide is a(n) _____-headed reptile named _____ . She is _____ and knows
                 number   exotic location   adjective

everything about the cave's formations and history. The area we're floating through is _____ years old
                                                                                        large number

and _____ formed when _____ repeatedly washed the rock away. And I thought
      adverb ending in –ly   something gooey

_____ took forever to do! We see _____ stalactites hanging from the ceiling, and our
   type of chore   adjective

tubes _____ around stalagmites rising from the ground. The river picks up speed as we get near
         verb

the end of the tour. We unhook our inner tubes, put on our _____ , and tumble over a(n)
                                                            clothing item, plural

_____-fall. Look out below, here comes my famous _____ !
   liquid   type of swim

31

friend's name

something smelly

adjective

adjective

favorite color

spicy food

adjective

verb ending in –ing

same friend's name

noun, plural

relative's name

verb ending in –s

animal

something gross, plural

noun, plural

body part, plural

adjective

same color

Time for a Dip!

"Phew. What a stink!" _____ exclaims as we arrive at the shore. There's a sign
                              friend's name

saying "_____ Springs." It's famous for its rocky shore and _____ water. The
        something smelly   adjective

geothermal activity of a(n) _____ volcano makes the water seem to glow shades of _____ .
                              adjective   favorite color

And the water is so warm I feel like a(n) _____ just dipping in my _____ toe.
                                            spicy food   adjective

Instead of _____ , _____ and I want to put our _____ up and relax.
            verb ending in –ing   same friend's name   noun, plural

It's hard to relax though, when the air smells like _____ 's feet after (s)he _____
                                                      relative's name   verb ending in –s

a marathon. We wave down a(n) _____ who is selling nose plugs and large _____
                                 animal   something gross, plural

on a stick. After putting on the nose plugs, we wrap _____ around our _____
                                                        noun, plural   body part, plural

and enjoy the steam of the _____ water. Time to get out of the water and continue our journey,
                             adjective

though. I hope this doesn't leave a(n) _____ glow on my skin.
                                         same color

first name beginning with "W"

word beginning with "R"

a profession

animal that lives underground

clothing item

noun

something gross

your hometown

verb ending in –ing

past-tense verb

verb

adjective

noun

something used for travel

noun

something old

pet's name

Fun Fact! NEW YORK CITY'S FIRST SUBWAY USED A GIANT FAN TO MOVE A CAR FORWARD AND BACKWARD.

Subway Surprise

I'm starting to wonder how we'll find our way out of this cave when I hear a *whoosh!* It's the sound of the cave's underground subway, the WORTS. WORTS stands for _____ 's Obviously _____
first name beginning with "W" · _word beginning with "R"_

Transportation System. It was named after its inventor: a hairy _____ _____
a profession · _animal that lives underground_

who was always in a hurry. We squeeze onboard next to a tall rat wearing a(n) _____ and carrying a
clothing item

miniature _____ . "Are you going to work?" we ask the rat. "Yes, I'm a professional _____
noun · _something gross_

taste-tester in _____ 's finest restaurant. When he asks why we're _____ down
your hometown · _verb ending in –ing_

here, I realize we totally _____ our science project! The rat suggests we _____
past-tense verb · _verb_

in an archaeological dig happening right now on the _____ side of the _____ . He
adjective · _noun_

pulls a(n) _____ out of his _____ to help us get there. He also hands us
something used for travel · _noun_

a(n) _____ to help pay the WORTS fare. I wish _____ was as well behaved as this rodent!
something old · _pet's name_

- friend's name
- shape
- adverb ending in –ly
- body part, plural
- kitchen utensil, plural
- verb ending in –ing
- same friend's name
- something slimy
- something enormous
- silly word
- same friend's name
- past-tense verb
- toy
- animal
- adjective
- something sticky
- noun, plural
- country

Fun Fact! THE **DINOSAUR** *VECTIDRACO DAISYMORRISAE* IS NAMED AFTER DAISY MORRIS, ITS **FOUR-YEAR-OLD** DISCOVERER.

Dig In!

_____ (friend's name) and I arrive at an archaeological site and the excavation crew immediately gives us the lowdown. They've roped off a(n) _____ (shape) -shaped site and are _____ (adverb ending in –ly) mapping every bit of it. So far, they've found several dinosaur _____ (body part, plural) and even a few petrified _____ (kitchen utensil, plural) . We each pick up a tool for _____ (verb ending in –ing) artifacts. _____ (same friend's name) uses a long _____ (something slimy) , while I carefully scrape the soil away with a scratchy _____ (something enormous) .

"_____ (silly word) !" _____ (same friend's name) shouts. "Look what I _____ (past-tense verb) !" (S)he holds up an ancient _____ (toy) . I uncover an inflatable _____ (animal) . It doesn't look old or very interesting, so I dig farther until something _____ (adjective) catches my eye. I change tools and use _____ (something sticky) to remove all the _____ (noun, plural) around my find. Whoa, it looks like a diamond the size of _____ (country) !

adjective

   friend's name

adjective

   adjective

jewelry, plural

   clothing item

your birthstone

   verb

noun

   adjective

adjective

   verb

math teacher's name

   noun, plural

royal title

   adjective

Fun Fact! **EARTHWORMS** ARE COVERED IN **SMALL HAIRS** THAT HELP THEM **BURROW** THROUGH DIRT.

Diamonds Are a Worm's Best Friend

Everyone will be so _____ when they see my diamond discovery! _____
                         adjective   friend's name

and I take it to a(n) _____ jewelry shop to learn more about it. Earthworms run the shop,
                      adjective

and they love gemstones, especially diamonds. They're decked out in _____ tiaras and emerald
                                                                      adjective

_____ . One worm is even wearing a(n) _____ made entirely of _____ .
jewelry, plural   clothing item   your birthstone

I'll have to ask him if I can _____ that for our class _____ next week! Clearly, these
                              verb   noun

worms have _____ taste, so it's no wonder they're in awe of my _____ find. They
            adjective   adjective

measure and study its every angle and edge. Then the worms _____ a giant calculator that would
                                                            verb

make _____ really jealous. After running the _____ , they tell me what
      math teacher's name   noun, plural

I found is actually a very rare diamond tooth from _____ Rex the Eighth. Not only can we use
                                                    royal title

this to ace our next science project, now we'll get _____ points in history class, too!
                                                     adjective

famous city

today's date

your name

verb ending in –s

adjective

friend's name

type of head wear, plural

noun, plural

same friend's name

noun

adjective

noun

favorite actor

adjective

verb

celebrity's name

verb

something odd, plural

Made for a Museum

When the mayor of underground _____ hears about my royal tooth, she proclaims
                                         famous city

_____ International _____ Day! The celebration _____ off with
     today's date   your name   verb ending in –s

a(n) _____ parade, and we're in it! _____ and I wear _____
         adjective   friend's name   type of head wear, plural

and toss _____ to the crowd. At a special ceremony, the mayor shows _____ and
            noun, plural   same friend's name

me a(n) _____ with both our names on it, and the title "Most _____ Explorers in Cave
             noun   adjective

History!" It's in the city's Hall of _____ between an autographed photo of _____ and
                                          noun   favorite actor

a(n) _____ empty space. The mayor points to the space and says, "That's where we'll _____
         adjective   verb

the tooth!" What? But how will I become rich and famous like _____ if the tooth is way
                                                                    celebrity's name

down here? Then I think about what a pain it would be to _____ it all the way home. We decide to
                                                               verb

check it out. Besides, it really completes the museum's collection of _____ .
                                                                           something odd, plural

friend's name

verb

adjective ending in –est

adverb ending in –ly

animal with a tail

adjective

adverb ending in –ly

adjective

body part

animal sound

something expensive

noun

verb

same friend's name

electronic gadget

sports equipment, plural

something silly

Fun Fact!

IN MEXICO'S
CAVE OF CRYSTALS
THE TEMPERATURE REACHES
112°F (44.4°C).

Magic Crystals

Not So Crystal Clear

_____ and I _____ into a room filled with the _____ crystals we've ever seen.
friend's name   verb   adjective ending in –est

I lean in _____ to one and see words written on it. Did a(n) _____ scribble these words
          adverb ending in –ly   animal with a tail

with its tail? Because they look like a(n) _____ mess. Nearby, we see a sign that explains these are magic
                                          adjective

crystals. Each one has special directions on it, and if we follow them _____ we'll be granted a wish.
                                                                        adverb ending in –ly

I quickly read over the _____ text on one crystal and get started. I spin on my _____ and
                        adjective   body part

hold my left foot above my head. Then I _____ like an animal and wish for a(n) _____ .
                                        animal sound   something expensive

Bang! A curly _____ appears on my head and I immediately _____ from its weight.
             noun   verb

_____ tries next and wishes for the newest _____ . Poof! A set of
same friend's name   electronic gadget

_____ appears. Good thing we didn't wish for _____ ! Since we can't
sports equipment, plural   something silly

seem to wish our way out, we're going to have to keep exploring.

measurement of time, plural

something cold, plural

adjective

noun

something sweet

friend's name

noun, plural

verb

type of building

adjective ending in –er

favorite flavor

salty food

noun, plural

large number

good smell

noun

verb ending in –s

noun

body part

Fun Fact! AN **ICE-CREAM SHOP** IN VENEZUELA SERVES **850 FLAVORS** —INCLUDING SQUID, MACARONI AND CHEESE, AND ROSE.

TODAY'S SPECIAL: BERRY POTTER

Brrr Cave

We've been walking for _____ , and suddenly it's gotten as cold as _____ .
_____measurement of time, plural_____   _____something cold, plural_____

The walls are covered in ice. *Brr!* But what's that _____ smell? Do I detect the hint of a(n)
_____adjective_____

_____ covered in _____ ? *Mmm.* _____ and I use his/her _____
_____noun_____   _____something sweet_____   _____friend's name_____   _____noun, plural_____

to _____ along the cave's slippery wall. Deep in a corner, we see bears working in an ice-cream
_____verb_____

_____ . If their ice cream smells this good, I'm sure it tastes even _____ . I always
_____type of building_____   _____adjective ending in –er_____

go with _____ , but the chocolate _____ sounds really yummy. This is going to be
_____favorite flavor_____   _____salty food_____

a tough choice! We pull up two _____ to sit on and ask for _____ scoops
_____noun, plural_____   _____large number_____

of _____ . The bear behind the counter grins and scoops the ice cream right from a(n)
_____good smell_____

_____ ! Talk about cool! We watch another bear making milk shakes. It _____ the
_____noun_____   _____verb ending in –s_____

ice cream in a(n) _____ with its furry _____ . I'm glad we didn't order that.
_____noun_____   _____body part_____

adjective

verb

friend's name

noun

adjective

local sports team

verb

adverb ending in –ly

number

noun

body part

type of transportation

verb

same type of transportation

plant

Fun Fact! A STAR-NOSED MOLE HAS 22 TENTACLES SURROUNDING ITS NOSE.

46

We've had a(n) _____ time exploring underground. But it's time to go home. We walk and
            adjective

walk ... but which way did we _____ in? _____ and I can't even remember how long
                              verb   _friend's name_

we've been down here. I knock on a nearby _____ and a(n) _____ mole wearing
                                          noun   _adjective_

a(n) _____ jersey answers. What luck! She says she can _____ us the way home.
     local sports team   _verb_

She begins to dig _____ through the soil, but she's not making much of a dent. At this rate,
                  adverb ending in –ly

it will take _____ years to get home. "Do you want a(n) _____ to help dig that tunnel to
             number   _noun_

the surface?" I ask her. "I'm not digging a tunnel," she says, shaking her _____ . "I was looking for
                                                                           body part

my _____ keys." She holds them up, and we all _____ into her _____ .
   type of transportation   _verb_   _same type of transportation_

In minutes, we pop up in the _____ garden in front of my house. With all the photos and
                             plant

stories from our journey, I know our science project is going to rock!

Credits

Cover, Andrew Zarivny/Shutterstock; 4, DS Design/Shutterstock; 6, Kojihirano/Shutterstock; 8, Farbled/Shutterstock; 10, TT Studio/Shutterstock; 12, Nature Capture Realfoto/Shutterstock; 14, Can Balcioglu/Shutterstock; 16, Salim October/Shutterstock; 18, Tutti Frutti/Shutterstock; 20, Evren Kalinbacak/Shutterstock; 22, hxdbzxy/Shutterstock; 24, Laura Stone/Shutterstock; 26, Joop Hoek/Shutterstock; 28, Vladislav/Shutterstock; 30, Jason Patrick Ross/Shutterstock; 32, Menno Schaefer/Shutterstock; 34, Pashin Georgiy/Shutterstock; 36, Irina Borsuchenko/Shutterstock; 38, Dotshock/Shutterstock; 40, TT Studio/Shutterstock; 42, Peter Gudella/Shutterstock; 44, Volodymyr Goinyk/Shutterstock.

Published by the National Geographic Society

Gary E. Knell, *President and Chief Executive Officer*
John M. Fahey, *Chairman of the Board*
Declan Moore, *Executive Vice President; President, Publishing and Travel*
Melina Gerosa Bellows, *Publisher; Chief Creative Officer, Books, Kids, and Family*

Prepared by the Book Division

Hector Sierra, *Senior Vice President and General Manager*
Nancy Laties Feresten, *Senior Vice President, Kids Publishing and Media*
Jennifer Emmett, *Vice President, Editorial Director, Kids Books*
Eva Absher-Schantz, *Design Director, Kids Publishing and Media*
Jay Sumner, *Director of Photography, Kids Publishing*
R. Gary Colbert, *Production Director*
Jennifer A. Thornton, *Director of Managing Editorial*

Staff for This Book

Shelby Alinsky, *Project Editor*
James Hiscott, Jr., *Art Director*
Kelley Miller, *Senior Photo Editor*
Kelley Miller, *Writer*
Kevin Rechin, *Illustrator*
Paige Towler, *Editorial Assistant*
Allie Allen, Sanjida Rashid, *Design Production Assistants*
Margaret Leist, *Photo Assistant*
Grace Hill, *Associate Managing Editor*
Joan Gossett, *Production Editor*
Lewis R. Bassford, *Production Manager*
Susan Borke, *Legal and Business Affairs*

Production Services

Phillip L. Schlosser, *Senior Vice President*
Chris Brown, *Vice President, NG Book Manufacturing*
George Bounelis, *Senior Production Manager*
Nicole Elliott, *Director of Production*
Rachel Faulise, *Manager*
Robert L. Barr, *Manager*

Editorial, Design, and Production by Plan B Book Packagers

The National Geographic Society is one of the world's largest nonprofit scientific and educational organizations. Founded in 1888 to "increase and diffuse geographic knowledge," the Society's mission is to inspire people to care about the planet. It reaches more than 400 million people worldwide each month through its official journal, *National Geographic*, and other magazines; National Geographic Channel; television documentaries; music; radio; films; books; DVDs; maps; exhibitions; live events; school publishing programs; interactive media; and merchandise. National Geographic has funded more than 10,000 scientific research, conservation, and exploration projects and supports an education program promoting geographic literacy.

For more information, please call 1-800-NGS LINE (647-5463) or write to the following address:

National Geographic Society, 1145 17th Street N.W., Washington, D.C. 20036-4688 U.S.A.

Visit us online at nationalgeographic.com/books

For librarians and teachers: ngchildrensbooks.org

More for kids from National Geographic: kids.nationalgeographic.com

For information about special discounts for bulk purchases, please contact National Geographic Books Special Sales: ngspecsales@ngs.org

For rights or permissions inquiries, please contact National Geographic Books Subsidiary Rights: ngbookrights@ngs.org

ISBN: 978-1-4263-1737-8

Printed in Hong Kong

14/THK/1